DEADLY ANIMALS
ULTIMATE TOP TENS

Natural History Consultant
Dr Kim Bryan Ph.D

WISE WALRUS

WISE WALRUS

First published in Great Britain in 2012 by Wise Walrus.
The Pantiles Chambers,
85 High Street, Tunbridge Wells,
Kent
TN1 1XP
United Kingdom
www.wisewalrus.co.uk

Design: Plum Pudding

ISBN 978-1-84898-426-4

Printed in China

A CIP catalogue record for this book is available from the British Library. No part of this publication may be reproduced, copied, stored in a retrieval system or transmitted in any form or by any means electronic, mechanical, photocopying, recording or otherwise without prior writtenc onsent of the copyright owner.

Picture credits (t=top; b=bottom, c=centre): Corbis: 36-37c, 60-61c, 66t, 70b, 76 all. © Craig Brown: 8-9c; © Dorling Kindersley: 5t; 16-17c. Dreamtime: 74-75t © Puddingpie. FLPA: 38-39b; 40 all; 48-49, 50-51; 59-59 c; 73t, 77 all. Natural History Photography: 42t-43 small. NHPL: 44-45 c; 52-53. © Sergey Krasovskiy 18-19. Shutterstock: 10-11 c, 24-25 c © Ralph Jürgen Kraft; 12-13 c © Linda Bucklin; 22-23 c © Catmando; 24-25 © Marques; 27 t © Elinag; 32-33 c © Peter Jochems; 32b © W. Scott; 4b; 31, 34-35c, 55, 56-57c; 64-65c; 66-67c © Eric Isselée; 34-35b © Dirk Ercken; 5b, 46-47 all © Kletr; 58-59 © Michael J Thompson; 62-63 c © Ludmila Yilmaz; 68-69 John Kasawa; 72-73c © Mike Price: 74-75; Ticktock Media Archive 8b; 10b;13t; 14-15 all; 17t; 19t; 20-21c; 23t; 26-27 c; 28-29 all. Wikipedia: 37t.

Every effort has been made to trace copyright holders and we apologise in advance for any omission. We would be pleased to insert the appropriate acknowledgements in any subsequent edition of this publication.

Contents

Introduction

Which animal wins the title of the *most deadly* of all time? It is not such an easy question as you might think. Does it belong to the fast and powerful big cats; or is it one of the ancient dinosaurs like Tyrannosaurus Rex or even a large marine predator, like the Great White Shark or the Killer Whale, as recent movies and various legends seem to suggest?

Maybe. Yet, sometimes small is powerful, especially if armed with stingers or fangs. Some of the tiniest creatures of all can claim the largest number of victims, like the Anopheles Mosquito, which can spread the deadly disease malaria...

So, it is really difficult to judge, isn't it? To help you make up your own mind, we have captured the most dangerous creatures on Earth within the pages of this book. Carefully open the crates, one by one, and start the deadly countdown.

Watch out, though! Whatever the overall score, all animals featured here are very dangerous! So study them really well, as the next time you meet them, it could also be the last!

WARNING. THINGS GET GRIM FROM HERE ON IN

Dinosaur Hunters
INTRODUCTION

The period of Earth's history between 245 and 65 million years ago is often known as the Age of Dinosaurs (see table on the right). There were thousands of different dinosaurs; most were peaceful herbivores, but some were ferocious, meat-eating predators. This section presents our Top Ten of the most dangerous dinosaurs, rated according to:

HUNTING

Meat-eating dinosaurs employed a wide variety of hunting techniques. Some were pack-hunters, while others lived and hunted alone. Some dinosaurs preferred to wait in ambush for their prey, while others were constantly on the prowl for something to eat. We based our scores on the overall efficiency of the technique that was most frequently employed.

JAW POWER

Most dinosaur predators relied entirely on their jaws for killing, as well as eating. We based our score on the size and strength of the jaws, together with the number, length and sharpness of the teeth. Only a few dinosaurs, such as our overall winner Deinonychus, had claws that were also efficient weapons, and they were awarded bonus points.

2 Tyrannosaurus Rex

TWO

This is the most famous of all the dinosaurs and one of the biggest land predators that has ever lived. It often is known as Tyrannosaurus Rex (or T Rex), because "rex" means "king" in Latin. It was first described in 1905 by an American geologist, Henry Fairfield Osborn.

JAW POWER

Tyrannosaurus had massive jaws with very powerful muscles and it could bite straight through even the biggest bones. Some of its teeth could reach 30 centimetres in length.

HUNTING

Tyrannosaurus probably stalked herds of plant-eating dinosaurs and picked off the weakest members.

BODY

Tyrannosaurus was 12 metres long and weighed more than 7,000 kilograms, but it had very puny little forelimbs that only grew to about 1 metre.

FACT: *T Rex was a very effective predator – thanks to its developed sense of smell and rather forward-facing eyes, which helped it judge distance.*

MOBILITY

High speed gives a predator a tremendous advantage – but speed alone is not everything. There is no point in being able to run faster than your prey, if you cannot change direction easily, or come to a sudden stop. Our dinosaur predators were given points for their speed, acceleration and agility, with extra points awarded to those with good jumping skills.

FRIGHT

Some of the meat-eating dinosaurs were as big as a bus – and any predator that size is frightening, especially if it is very close! The largest dinosaurs were not always the scariest, though, as they could often move rather slowly. We based our fright score on other features as well, such as jaw power, teeth length, hunting technique...

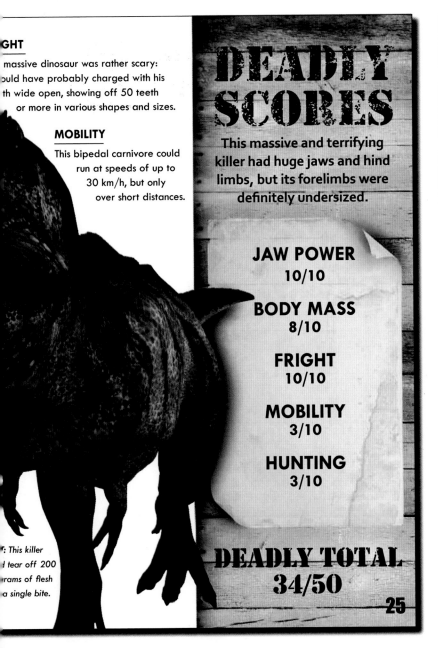

...GHT

massive dinosaur was rather scary: ...uld have probably charged with his ...th wide open, showing off 50 teeth or more in various shapes and sizes.

MOBILITY

This bipedal carnivore could run at speeds of up to 30 km/h, but only over short distances.

...: This killer ...d tear off 200 ...rams of flesh ...a single bite.

DEADLY SCORES

This massive and terrifying killer had huge jaws and hind limbs, but its forelimbs were definitely undersized.

JAW POWER
10/10

BODY MASS
8/10

FRIGHT
10/10

MOBILITY
3/10

HUNTING
3/10

DEADLY TOTAL
34/50

TRIASSIC 245.5-199.5 million years ago	
JURASSIC 199.5-145.5 million years ago	
CRETACEOUS 145.5-65.5 million years ago	

The Age of the Dinosaurs

BODY MASS

Size was obviously important for a dinosaur predator. The bigger the predator, the bigger the prey it can attack. Similarly with weight, a heavy predator will find it easier to drag down and overpower its prey. We gave our dinosaurs a combined score based on their size and weight, but in each case we also took into consideration the average size of their prey.

Dilophosaurus

Dilophosaurus lived during the early part of the Jurassic period. This carnivore had a distinctive crest made up of two bony ridges along the top of its skull. It is believed that this strip could have been used for communication or for mating displays. The fossil remains of Dilophosaurus were discovered in 1942 in Arizona, USA, by the palaeontologist Samuel Welles.

HUNTING

Most scientists believe that Dilophosaurus hunted in packs, so it could attack animals much larger than itself. Some scientists, however, think that Dilophosaurus fed only on carrion, i.e. carcasses of dead animals.

FACT: *Dilophosaurus had an unusually long tail for an active predator.*

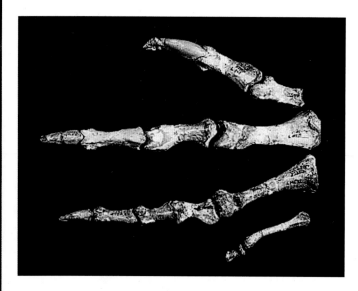

FACT: *The claws at the ends of the fingers and toes were very sharp, but at just a few centimetres long they were much shorter than those of other deadly predators of the time.*

BODY MASS

Dilophosaurus was about six metres in length and weighed about 500 kilograms. It had a slender build but was a ferocious fighter.

FRIGHT

Dilophosaurus was big enough to look scary, but those jaws were not as strong as they looked. Its claws were deadly.

JAW POWER

Although Dilophosaurus' jaws were packed with long sharp teeth, they were fairly weak.

MOBILITY

Dilophosaurus was a bipedal animal that hunted by chasing its prey. Powerful muscles in the hind limbs enabled it to run quickly.

DEADLY SCORES

This dinosaur just manages to get into our top ten because of its high score for mobility.

JAW POWER
1/10

BODY MASS
3/10

FRIGHT
3/10

MOBILITY
7/10

HUNTING
4/10

DEADLY TOTAL
18/50

Velociraptor

Velociraptor was a feathered dinosaur that lived in Asia towards the end of the Cretaceous period. The first remains were discovered in Mongolia by Henry Osborn in 1924. Velociraptor had a winning combination of speed, aggression and fearsome weapons – only its small size prevents it from being the overall winner. It was the size of a small turkey!

JAW POWER

It had about 80 teeth that were designed for ripping and tearing flesh. Narrow jaws allowed Velociraptor to push its head inside the carcass of a dinosaur.

HUNTING

Velociraptor was a pack hunter and a highly efficient predator. It attacked with the claws of all four limbs and could even jump up onto the back of its prey.

FRIGHT

Velociraptor was not very large, but it always hunted in a pack, clearly displaying its vicious 6.5 cm sickle-shaped claws, retracted from the ground, which it used to tear into its prey.

MOBILITY

Velociraptor was a fast-running bipedal dinosaur, capable of reaching speeds of 65 km/h. Its name means "speedy thief".

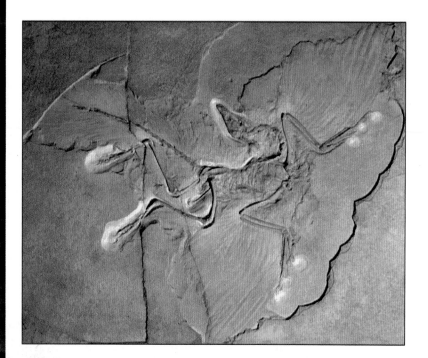

FACT: About 12 Velociraptor fossils have been found so far. One is thought to have died whilst fighting a Protoceratops.

BODY MASS

An average Velociraptor would have been about 2 metres long and just a metre tall at the hip. This dinosaur would have weighed about 20-25 kilograms.

FACT: *Velociraptor was one of the fastest and fiercest predators that ever lived.*

DEADLY SCORES

Too small to be more highly rated on an individual basis, but a pack of them would be a different matter.

JAW POWER
2/10

BODY MASS
1/10

FRIGHT
1/10

MOBILITY
10/10

HUNTING
8/10

DEADLY TOTAL
22/50

Giganotosaurus

Giganotosaurus is one of the largest carnivores that ever walked the Earth. It is also one of the most mysterious of the meat-eating dinosaurs because it was not discovered until 1993. An amateur fossil-hunter called Ruben Carolini made the discovery in Patagonia, Argentina.

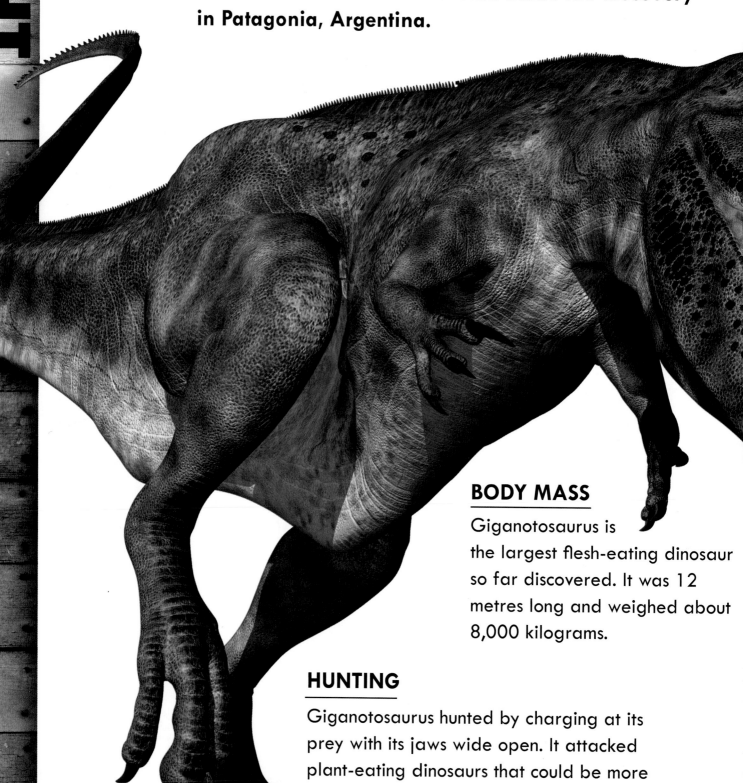

BODY MASS

Giganotosaurus is the largest flesh-eating dinosaur so far discovered. It was 12 metres long and weighed about 8,000 kilograms.

HUNTING

Giganotosaurus hunted by charging at its prey with its jaws wide open. It attacked plant-eating dinosaurs that could be more than 20 metres in length.

FACT: *The skull of the largest specimen had a length of 195 cm, but it still housed a very small brain.*

JAW POWER

The jaws were crammed with narrow, pointed teeth that had serrated edges for slicing through flesh. The biggest teeth were about 20 centimetres long.

FACT: *Giganotosaurus was capable of attacking and killing even large dinosaurs.*

FRIGHT

Giganotosaurus was huge – bigger than Tyrannosaurus Rex , although smaller than the largest Spinosaurus – and looked very scary, but fortunately it seems to have been quite a rare dinosaur.

MOBILITY

or such a large animal, Giganotosaurus could un surprisingly quickly at up to 24 km/h. Its im, pointed tail may have provided balance nd quick turning when it was running.

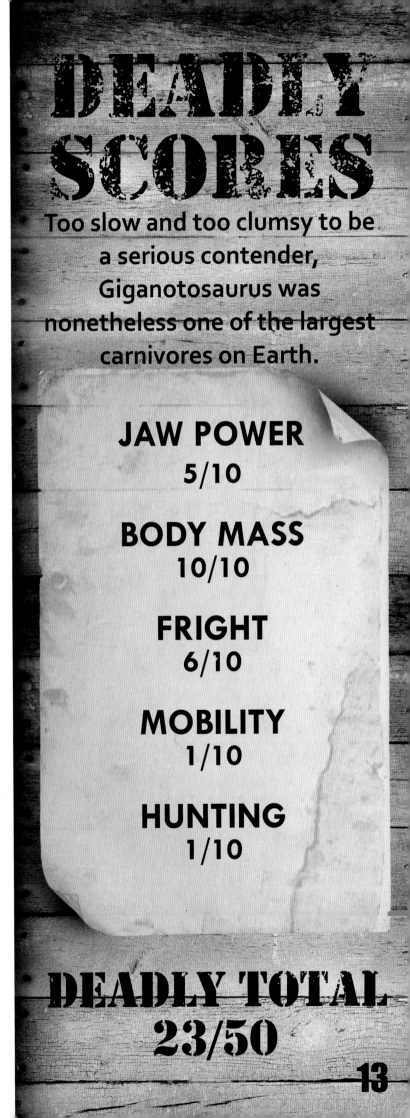

DEADLY SCORES

Too slow and too clumsy to be a serious contender, Giganotosaurus was nonetheless one of the largest carnivores on Earth.

JAW POWER
5/10

BODY MASS
10/10

FRIGHT
6/10

MOBILITY
1/10

HUNTING
1/10

DEADLY TOTAL
23/50

Troodon

Troodon was a small bipedal dinosaur that lived at the very end of the Cretaceous period. In terms of brain size to body weight, it may have been the brainiest animal on Earth at that time. The first Troodon fossil was discovered by Ferdinand V. Hayden in 1855. The US palaeontologist Joseph Leidy named the species in 1856.

JAW POWER

This dinosaur had up to 120 curved teeth packed into its mouth. Each tooth had a wide, serrated edge for slicing through flesh.

BODY MASS

Troodon was about 3 metr long and weighed 40-50 kilograms. It would probal have been covered in feathers.

MOBILITY

Long legs and light body weight allowed Troodon to take very big strides, so it could run extremely quickly – possibly faster than any other dinosaur.

FACT: *In terms of overall body-shape, Troodon was very similar to a present-day ostrich.*

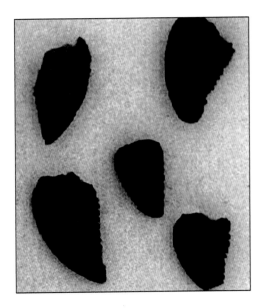

FACT: *These curved teeth are responsible for the name Troodon, which means "wounding tooth".*

DEADLY SCORES

Very fast, but a lightweight dinosaur that was only really scary at night.

JAW POWER
3/10

BODY MASS
2/10

FRIGHT
2/10

MOBILITY
9/10

HUNTING
9/10

DEADLY TOTAL
25/50

HUNTING

Forward-facing eyes gave the Troodon good binocular vision, ideal to judge distance and chase small mammals, birds, lizards and snakes. The large size of the eyes allowed the pursuit even in low light conditions, either at night, dawn or dusk.

FRIGHT

It was too small to be very scary during the day, but thanks to its good night vision, it could take its prey by surprise in dim light.

Carcharodonto

During the middle part of the Cretaceous period, this dinosaur was the top predator in North Africa. It had razor-sharp teeth and it was big enough to attack and kill the largest plant-eating dinosaurs. First discovered in Algeria in 1927 and erroneously called Megalosaurus saharicus, it adopted its current name in 1931. The first fossils were destroyed during World War II, but more were found in the 1990s.

JAW POWER

This dinosaur had wide, powerful jaws the size of a human, with sharp teeth that could easily penetrate the toughest skin.

BODY MASS

Carcharodontosaurus grew up to 11 metres in length – nearly as big as Giganotosaurus – and weighed more than 7,000 kilograms.

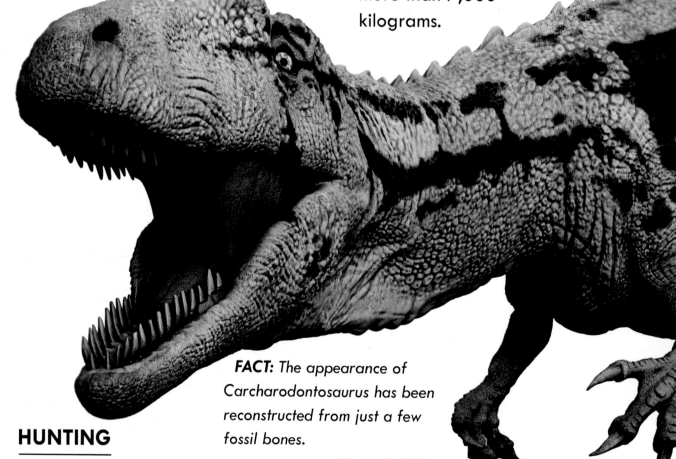

FACT: The appearance of Carcharodontosaurus has been reconstructed from just a few fossil bones.

HUNTING

Carcharodontosaurus was probably an ambush hunter that waited in hiding until it could launch a surprise attack.

MOBILITY

Carcharodontosaurus was bipedal, but it relied on power and weight rather than speed and it could not run very quickly.

...aurus

FACT: *Carcharodontosaurus' skull is massive, especially when compared to a human skull.*

FRIGHT

This dinosaur was big and very fierce, but it was also quite slow moving, so the prey could probably manage to run away if they spotted it in time.

DEADLY SCORES

Low scores for speed and hunting are responsible for this giant killer not being more highly rated.

JAW POWER
4/10

BODY MASS
9/10

FRIGHT
9/10

MOBILITY
2/10

HUNTING
2/10

DEADLY TOTAL
26/50

Albertosaurus

Albertosaurus was a sleek, saw-toothed predator that hunted Hadrosaurs and other plant-eating dinosaurs. It lived in North America during the last part of the Cretaceous period. Geologist Joseph Tyrrell discovered fossils of Albertosaurus in 1884 in Alberta, Canada.

JAW POWER

Albertosaurus had a big head, with large, powerful jaws. There were about 36 razor-sharp teeth in its upper jaw and about 30 in the lower jaw.

HUNTING

Albertosaurus may not have been a very good hunter, because its eyes were positioned at the side of its head. Predators see better when their eyes are at the front.

FRIGHT

This was a very scary dinosaur because it combined large size with fast speed, which made it a deadly hunter.

FACT: *This skull still has most of the teeth intact.*

BODY MASS

Albertosaurus measured
9 metres in length, stood
4 metres high at the hip
and weighed about
3,000 kilograms.

MOBILITY

This large bipedal dinosaur
may have reached 30 km/h
when running at top speed,
as fast as any other dinosaur
of its size.

FACT: *Like other bipedal dinosaurs,*
Albertosaurus used its tail for balance.

DEADLY SCORES

This was a big, fast predator,
but there were other dinosaurs
that were bigger and faster.

JAW POWER
8/10

BODY MASS
5/10

FRIGHT
4/10

MOBILITY
6/10

HUNTING
5/10

DEADLY TOTAL
28/50

Allosaurus

Allosaurus was one of the the largest predators on Earth. It lived between the end of the Jurassic period and the beginning of the Cretaceous period. The first fossils were described in 1877 in Wyoming, USA, by the famous fossil-hunter Othniel C. Marsh.

JAW POWER

Allosaurus had about 70 sharp teeth and each tooth was up to 10 centimetres long. But the teeth were fragile and broke off easily.

BODY MASS

Allosaurus was about 7.5 metres long when fully grown. Some specimens of this giant could weigh up to 2000 kilograms or even more.

HUNTING

Allosaurus may have hunted in packs, using the 25-centimetre claws on its forelimbs to slash open its prey.

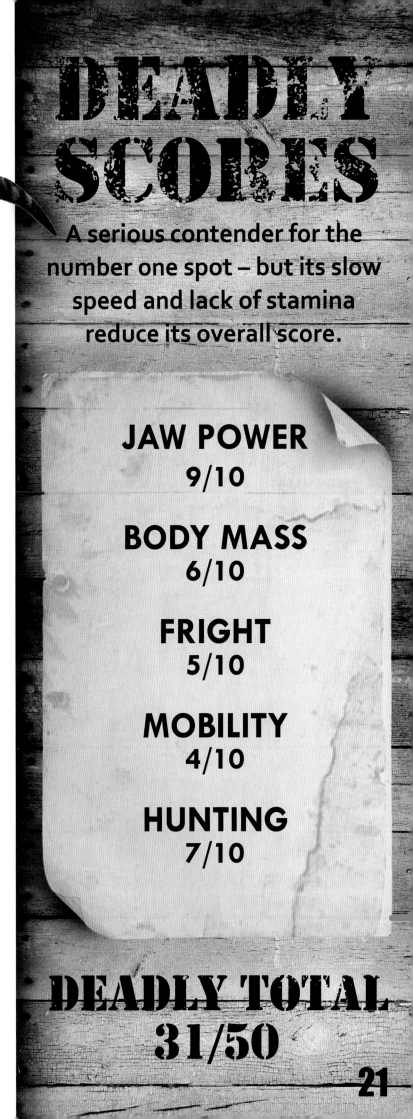

FACT: Allosaurus was a top predator with no natural enemies.

FACT: Allosaurus was capable of killing even the biggest plant-eating dinosaurs.

MOBILITY

This bipedal carnivore may have reached a top speed of about 19 km/h, but it had no stamina for a long chase.

FRIGHT

This dinosaur was even bigger and more aggressive than Albertosaurus and didn't have a problem in attacking large herbivores or even other predators.

DEADLY SCORES

A serious contender for the number one spot – but its slow speed and lack of stamina reduce its overall score.

JAW POWER
9/10

BODY MASS
6/10

FRIGHT
5/10

MOBILITY
4/10

HUNTING
7/10

DEADLY TOTAL
31/50

Spinosaurus

Spinosaurus was a fierce predator that lived in Africa during the mid Cretaceous period. It had a strange 1.5-metre tall crest along its back that was made of long spines covered by tough skin. The first fossil of Spinosaurus was discovered in Egypt in 1912 by German palaeontologist Ernst Stromer.

JAW POWER

This dinosaur had long, narrow jaws lined with razor-sharp, pointed teeth.

FRIGHT

The sight of this dinosaur was enough to give nightmares, it was indeed a gigantic heavyweight killer with jaws like a crocodile.

FACT: Like many other dinosaurs of the same era, Spinosaurus sported a crest, or sail, on its back: it was probably used to regulate its body temperature.

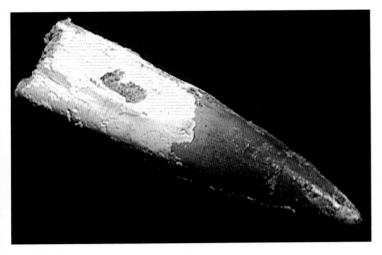

FACT: Each tooth was designed to penetrate deeply into the prey's flesh.

HUNTING

The design of the jaws and teeth suggest that Spinosaurus probably fed mainly on fish that it snatched from rivers and lakes.

BODY MASS

Spinosaurus reached lengths of up to 16 metres and weighed up to 7,000 kilograms.

MOBILITY

The longer than usual forelimbs suggest that Spinosaurus may have walked on all fours at least some of the time.

DEADLY SCORES

Spinosaurus was large and fierce – for a fish-eater – but a bit too slow to score any higher.

JAW POWER
6/10

BODY MASS
7/10

FRIGHT
8/10

MOBILITY
5/10

HUNTING
6/10

DEADLY TOTAL
32/50

Tyrannosaurus Rex

This is the most famous of all the dinosaurs and one of the biggest land predators that has ever lived. It often is known as Tyrannosaurus Rex (or T Rex), because "rex" means "king" in Latin. It was first described in 1905 by an American geologist, Henry Fairfield Osborn.

JAW POWER

Tyrannosaurus had massive jaws with very powerful muscles and it could bite straight through even the biggest bones. Some of its teeth could reach 30 centimetres in length.

HUNTING

Tyrannosaurus probably stalked herds of plant-eating dinosaurs and picked off the weakest members.

BODY

Tyrannosaurus was 12 metres long and weighed more than 7,000 kilograms, but it had very puny little forelimbs that only grew to about 1 metre.

FACT: T Rex was a very effective predator — thanks to its developed sense of smell and rather forward-facing eyes, which helped it judge distance.

FRIGHT

This massive dinosaur was rather scary: it would have probably charged with his mouth wide open, showing off 50 teeth or more in various shapes and sizes.

MOBILITY

This bipedal carnivore could run at speeds of up to 30 km/h, but only over short distances.

FACT: *This killer could tear off 200 kilograms of flesh with a single bite.*

DEADLY SCORES

This massive and terrifying killer had huge jaws and hind limbs, but its forelimbs were definitely undersized.

JAW POWER
10/10

BODY MASS
8/10

FRIGHT
10/10

MOBILITY
3/10

HUNTING
3/10

DEADLY TOTAL
34/50

Deinonychus

Deinonychus was the supreme dinosaur predator – a fast and deadly pack hunter. It lived in North America during the early part of the Cretaceous period. Remains of Deinonychus were discovered in 1931 in Montana, USA, by fossil hunter – Barnum Brown but it was only described in 1969 by US palaeontologist John Ostrom.

FRIGHT

Just one of these dinosaurs was scary, and no animal stood a chance against a whole pack of these vicious killers as they could jump on the back of their prey and tear their flesh with both claws and teeth.

BODY MASS

Deinonychus was a medium-sized carnivore that weighed about 80 kilograms and stood about 1.5 metres tall.

HUNTING

Its hind limbs were equipped with long, vicious claws that were capable of hanging onto and ripping open the flesh of the largest prey.

FACT: *Although Deinonychus was no taller than a human being, it carried an incredible amount of killing power.*

FACT: *Each tooth could cut through skin and muscle like the blade of a knife.*

JAW POWER

A combination of powerful jaw muscles and curved teeth with serrated edges meant that Deinonychus could bite off huge chunks of flesh.

MOBILITY

Being so light, Deinonychus was a fast-running, agile predator that could attack with the claws of all four limbs as well as its teeth.

DEADLY SCORES

Among the fastest, fiercest and most fearsome – this dinosaur is enough to give even a Tyrannosaurus bad dreams.

JAW POWER
7/10

BODY MASS
4/10

FRIGHT
7/10

MOBILITY
8/10

HUNTING
10/10

DEADLY TOTAL
36/50

CLOSE, BUT NOT CLOSE ENOUGH

Before deciding our Top Ten Dinosaurs, we also considered these animals – all of them were deadly killers, but not quite deadly enough to make the Top Ten.

HERRERASAURUS

Herrerasaurus was one of the very first meat-eating theropod dinosaurs. It lived in South America about 225 million years ago during the Triassic period. Herrerasaurus was about three metres long and weighed about 200 kilograms. It walked and ran on its hind legs, and would have hunted small and medium-sized plant-eating dinosaurs, such as Pisanosaurus.

COELOPHYSIS

Coelophysis was a vicious pack-hunter that lived in North America during the late Triassic period. This small theropod dinosaur was about 3 metres long, but weighed just 25 kilograms. Hundreds of Coelophysis fossils were discovered at Ghost Ranch in New Mexico, USA, in the 1940s. Analysis of the fossils revealed that Coelophysis was a cannibal that sometimes ate its own kind. This has since been disputed.

BARYONYX

Baryonyx was a slightly smaller relative of Spinosaurus that lived in Europe and Africa about 120 million years ago. It measured about 10 metres in length and weighed about 2,000 kilograms. Like its larger relative, Baryonyx was a bipedal dinosaur that probably specialised in hunting fish, snatching them out of the water with its long jaws.

COMPSOGNATHUS

Compsognathus was one of the smallest known dinosaurs. It measured just 90 centimetres and most of the length was in the tail. That did not stop it from being an agile and efficient predator. This tiny theropod was only about the size of a chicken and lived during the middle of the Jurassic period. Compsognathus was bipedal and used the claws on its forefeet to hold its prey while it bit off chunks of flesh.

STRUTHIOMIMUS

This fast, bipedal omnivore lived in North America about 75 million years ago. Its name means "ostrich mimic" and, like the present-day ostrich, this theropod dinosaur ate anything that it could find. Struthiomimus had large eyes at the sides of its head, and was constantly on the alert for danger. When threatened by larger predators, Struthiomimus could run away at speeds of up to 65 km/h.

Lethal Killers
INTRODUCTION

This section is a catalogue of the world's most deadly living creatures. There are many dangerous animals around the world, and many of them can cause injury, and even death. But most of them are just dangerous because they are large or have sharp teeth. The creatures in this book are different – they are not just dangerous, they are real killers, one and all. Our Top Ten deadly creatures were rated according to:

PREY

Here, the focus is on what these deadly creatures eat – even if, as with the stonefish, they do not actually use their deadly characteristics while hunting. We looked at the size and variety of prey, and we also considered whether the prey was easy or difficult to locate.

DANGER

For this category we looked at all the features that make a particular animal dangerous and gave them separate scores. We also considered whether the animal is aggressive (which increases its danger score), how widely it is distributed, and whether it is common or rare.

8 EIGHT Sydney Funnel-Web Spider

The funnel-web spider that lives around the city of Sydney in Australia is probably the most dangerous spider on Earth. Although it mainly lives in the woodland surrounding the city, the Sydney funnel-web spider is often found in garages and backyards, and even underneath the floors of houses.

SHAPE
The Sydney funnel-web is quite large for a spider, with a body length of anything from 2-7 centimetres. Males are more lightly built than females and their venom is stronger.

ATTACK
The male feeds by lying in wait at the entrance of its burrow. It lays silk threads around the entrance and, as soon as the prey touches them, the spider feels the vibration and rushes out to bite its victim.

FACT: When threatened, this spider raises its head and forelegs to look more menacing and give a warning.

SHAPE

When studying deadly creatures, it soon became clear that size was not particularly important. Instead, we gave points for complexity of shape – the animals with the most complex shapes were awarded the most points. A more complicated shape can in fact make a creature more difficult to recognize and avoid. Its shape may also give the creature an increased opportunity for attack.

LETHAL POWER

This category is only concerned with the physical effects of the venom, toxin or other substances that causes death. Wherever possible, records of attacks on human beings were examined, and the lethality of the substance expressed in terms of human deaths. The effects on any intended prey, which is generally much smaller than a human being, can be considered as the same.

CT: *These spiders are dark brown in* ·*our, and live in funnel-shaped burrows.*

·ANGER

·ost spiders have venom that is too weak · affect large animals. The Sydney funnel-·eb spider is unusual because its venom · super-deadly to human beings, and its ·arp fangs can penetrate clothing.

·ETHAL POWER

·e Sydney funnel-web spider has its ·wn unique venom. Once it gets into ·e bloodstream, it begins to attack ·e heart and can cause death in a period ranging between 15 minutes and 3 days.

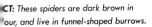

PREY

This spider will attack humans if it feels threatened, but it mainly eats snails, small amphibians, beetles and cockroaches. They even eat small lizards.

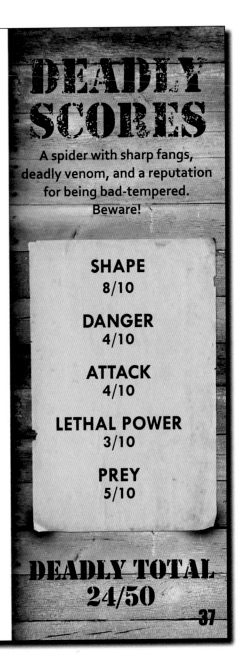

DEADLY SCORES

A spider with sharp fangs, deadly venom, and a reputation for being bad-tempered. Beware!

SHAPE
8/10

DANGER
4/10

ATTACK
4/10

LETHAL POWER
3/10

PREY
5/10

DEADLY TOTAL
24/50

ATTACK

Here we examined the animal's mode of attack and the actual process by which it kills its victims. Animals that employ an unusual method of attack scored higher than those that set upon their prey in a similar way to many other creatures. Additional points were given to those deadly creatures that take their victims by surprise.

Piranha

This fish has earned its nickname of the "Wolf of the Waters". It has sharp teeth, hunts in groups and has a voracious appetite for meat. One piranha will give you a nasty bite, but a group of starving piranhas could devour even larger animals. The piranha is found in the Amazon and other rivers in South America.

ATTACK

Piranhas do not kill their prey, they just start eating it alive! Their teeth are triangular in shape and are razor sharp.

DANGER

The piranha has a superb sense of smell and can detect blood in the water from more than 1.5 km away. It lives in shoals of 100 or so fish that can all attack at the same time.

SHAPE

The average length is about 30 centimetres, but a well-fed piranha can reach twice that size.

PREY

The piranha normally eats fish, crabs and small mammals, but can devour even large animals within minutes.

FACT: The myth of the piranhas' feeding frenzy derives from an event organised in the early 1900: hordes of starving piranhas were tossed in a river and fed a bleeding cow. The fish attacked the animal reducing it to the bare bones.

FACT: The teeth of the piranha are specialised flesh slicers.

LETHAL POWER

The legend around this type of fish has exaggerated their lethal power: recent research suggests that they are not really a threat to humans and livestock

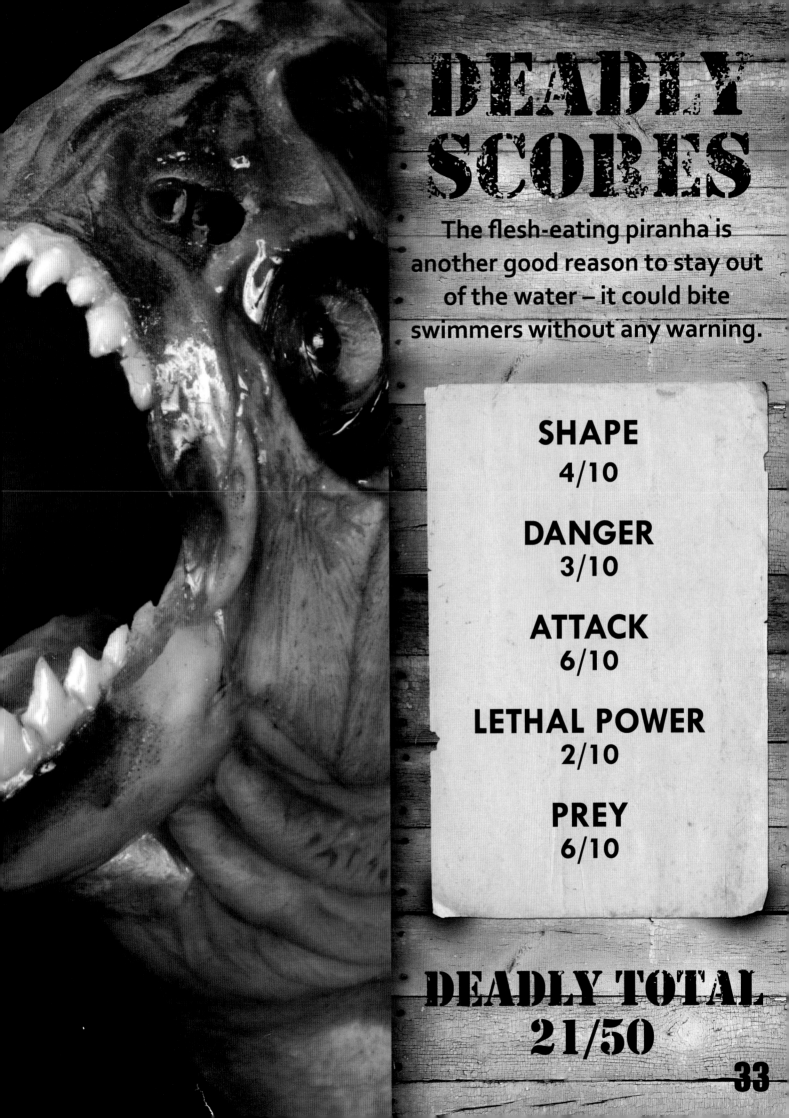

DEADLY SCORES

The flesh-eating piranha is another good reason to stay out of the water – it could bite swimmers without any warning.

SHAPE
4/10

DANGER
3/10

ATTACK
6/10

LETHAL POWER
2/10

PREY
6/10

DEADLY TOTAL
21/50

Poison Dart Frog

Most people think that small frogs are harmless, but the poison dart frog would prove them wrong! This frog lives in the tropical rain forests of Central and South America. Native people sometimes smear the frog's poison on the tips of their arrows and blowpipe darts when they go hunting.

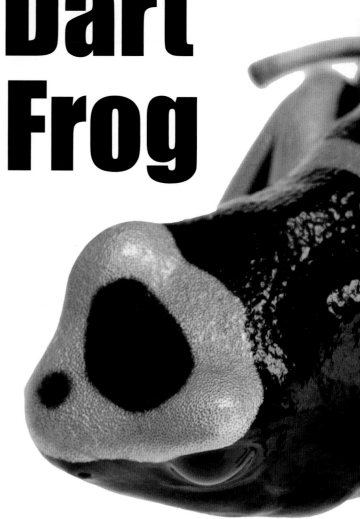

LETHAL POWER

Its glands produce a toxin that stops muscles from working and causes death. Just touching a poison frog can transfer enough toxin to kill an adult human being.

SHAPE

The poison dart frog ranges in size from just over 2 centimetres (the Strawberry Poison Dart Frog) to 6 centimetres (Dyeing Poison Frog).

FACT: The frog's bright coloration is a vivid warning: do not touch!

PREY

This frog mainly feeds on insects, especially ants, wh it needs to eat in order to produce its toxin.

DANGER

This small amphibian uses poison as a defence mechanism. Their bright colours warn predators that they are definitely not good to eat.

This frog is small, attractive and deadly. If you see one, do not be tempted to touch it.

SHAPE
3/10

DANGER
5/10

ATTACK
5/10

LETHAL POWER
7/10

PREY
3/10

FACT: *The skin of the poison dart frog is coated with poisonous slime.*

ATTACK

A thin layer of deadly poisonous slime covers the poison dart frog. The slime oozes from small glands in the frog's skin.

DEADLY TOTAL
23/50

Sydney Funnel-Web Spider

The funnel-web spider that lives around the city of Sydney in Australia is probably the most dangerous spider on Earth. Although it mainly lives in the woodland surrounding the city, the Sydney funnel-web spider is often found in garages and backyards, and even underneath the floors of houses.

SHAPE

The Sydney funnel-web is quite large for a spider, with a body length of anything from 2-7 centimetres. Males are more lightly built than females and their venom is stronger.

ATTACK

The male feeds by lying in wait at the entrance of its burrow. It lays silk threads around the entrance and, as soon as the prey touches them, the spider feels the vibration and rushes out to bite its victim.

FACT: *When threatened, this spider raises its head and forelegs to look more menacing and give a warning.*

FACT: These spiders are dark brown in colour, and live in funnel-shaped burrows.

DANGER

Most spiders have venom that is too weak to affect large animals. The Sydney funnel-web spider is unusual because its venom is super-deadly to human beings, and its sharp fangs can penetrate clothing.

LETHAL POWER

The Sydney funnel-web spider has its own unique venom. Once it gets into the bloodstream, it begins to attack the heart and can cause death in a period ranging between 15 minutes and 3 days.

PREY

This spider will attack humans if it feels threatened, but it mainly eats snails, small amphibians, beetles and cockroaches. They even eat small lizards.

DEADLY SCORES

A spider with sharp fangs, deadly venom, and a reputation for being bad-tempered. Beware!

SHAPE
8/10

DANGER
4/10

ATTACK
4/10

LETHAL POWER
3/10

PREY
5/10

DEADLY TOTAL
24/50

Blue-Ringed Octopus

The blue-ringed octopus is not only one of the most beautiful of all sea creatures – it is also one of the most deadly. This small, shy animal lives around coral reefs in the Indian and Pacific Oceans. Swimmers and divers have learned not to go looking for it because it has a very nasty bite.

SHAPE

Like all octopi, this one has a soft body with eight arms. The blue-ringed octopus is only about 15-20 centimetres long – about the size of a tennis ball.

LETHAL POWER

At first the bite feels like a bee-sting. Then the victim is completely paralysed and dies. There is no known antidote for the neurotoxin of the blue-ringed octopus.

DANGER

The blue-ringed octopus is the only octopus that has a venomous bite. People swimming in the sea that accidentally disturb this octopus are likely to get bitten with lethal results.

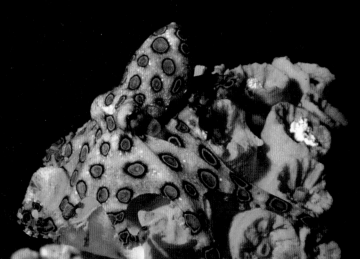

FACT: *The blue rings are a warning that the octopus is angry or frightened – in either case it may bite.*

PREY

This octopus feeds mainly on crabs and wounded fish that cannot swim away quickly.

FACT: A blue-ringed octopus weighs about 30 grams.

ATTACK

The octopus has a sharp beak that can slice into flesh. This allows its venomous saliva to flow into the wound.

DEADLY SCORES

A beautiful but deadly animal that is active during the day, which is when most people go swimming – make sure you take care in the water!

SHAPE
6/10

DANGER
5/10

ATTACK
6/10

LETHAL POWER
5/10

PREY
6/10

DEADLY TOTAL 28/50

6 Stonefish

Meet the fish that looks just like a rock — the stonefish, which lives around the coasts of the Indian and Pacific Oceans. Not only is it very ugly, it is also extremely dangerous, because it is the most venomous fish in the sea. Its sharp spines can easily penetrate flesh and inject their deadly venom.

SHAPE

A stonefish can grow up to 60 centimetres in length, with lumpy skin as camouflage that helps disguise its shape.

LETHAL POWER

If you step on a stonefish, it will start to hurt straight away and the pain will rapidly get worse. Some victims die within a few hours.

PREY

The stonefish only uses its spines for defence. It waits for shrimp and small fish to pass by, then strikes, gulping them down in under a second.

FACT: *The dorsal spines are connected to glands that expel an amount of venom depending on how much they are pressed. A few weeks pass before the glands regenerate and recharge.*

DANGER

The stonefish likes to lie half buried on the seabed waiting in ambush for its prey. People paddling or swimming in the sea sometimes step on a camouflaged stonefish by accident.

FACT: *A stonefish does not swim away when disturbed, it turns to face the intruder.*

ATTACK

There are 13 sharp, hollow spines in the fin running along the stonefish's back. Each of these spines can inject a deadly dose of venom.

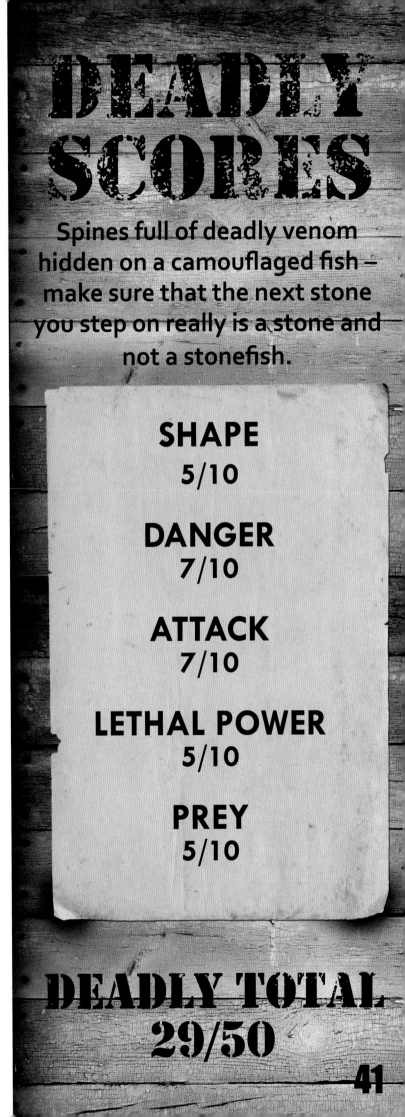

DEADLY SCORES

Spines full of deadly venom hidden on a camouflaged fish – make sure that the next stone you step on really is a stone and not a stonefish.

SHAPE
5/10

DANGER
7/10

ATTACK
7/10

LETHAL POWER
5/10

PREY
5/10

DEADLY TOTAL
29/50

5 Palestine Scorpion

The Palestine scorpion is the most dangerous scorpion in the world. It is found in the deserts and scrubland of the Middle East and North Africa. The Palestine scorpion is so deadly that local people have given it the name "Deathstalker".

SHAPE

The Palestine scorpion measures between 3 and 7.7 centimetres and presents two large pincers and a deadly tail sting.

PREY

It hunts insects but does not use its sting; instead it tears its prey apart with its pincer

LETHAL POWER

One drop of the venom is enough to kill an animal much larger than itself. Fortunately, scientists have developed an antidote for the sting of the Palestine scorpion.

FACT: Yellow coloration helps the scorpion to hide in desert sand.

ATTACK

The sharp sting penetrates flesh and injects deadly venom. The Palestine scorpion will sometimes sting a victim over and over again.

DANGER

This monster often hides under rocks or among loose sand and stones. If disturbed it will lash out with its deadly tail. Children are often stung while playing or walking to and from school.

FACT: The sting at the end the Deathstalker's curving tail carries a load of deadly venom.

The Palestine scorpion lives up to its nickname – Deathstalker – so stay away from the desert.

SHAPE
7/10

DANGER
8/10

ATTACK
4/10

LETHAL POWER
9/10

PREY
4/10

DEADLY TOTAL
32/50

Fierce Snake

The fierce snake is not as famous as cobras and rattlesnakes, but it is much more dangerous because it has the deadliest venom of any land snake. The fierce snake, which is also known as the Inland Taipan, is only found in central and northern Australia where it is very rare. The first live specimen was not captured until 1975.

DANGER

The fierce snake is shy, rare and usually docile, but if you are unlucky enough to see one, walk slowly away, because it can be very aggressive if disturbed.

ATTACK

This snake can strike faster than the eye can follow. As it bites its victim, two hollow fangs inject a small dose of its venom.

LETHAL POWER

This creature has the most toxic venom of any land snake. The fierce snake carries enough poison to kill about 250,000 mice, or about 100 adult humans.

SHAPE

The fierce snake grows up to 2.5 metres long. Its smooth body is brown in colour with a mustard-yellow belly and a glossy black head.

PREY

The fierce snake mainly hunts and eats small mammals, such as native rats and mice, which it swallows whole. Prey normally dies within seconds.

FACT: *The fierce snake strikes repeatedly at its prey, injecting venom each time.*

DEADLY SCORES

How can you rate the world's deadliest land snake? Fortunately for humans, the fierce snake is very rare.

SHAPE
6/10

DANGER
6/10

ATTACK
8/10

LETHAL POWER
9/10

PREY
6/10

FACT: *The fierce snake has enough deadly venom to kill 100 people.*

DEADLY TOTAL
35/50

Anopheles Mosquito

FACT: Female mosquitoes must drink blood in order to lay eggs.

"Mosquito" is a Portuguese word meaning "little fly" and its use dates back to about 1583. The female mosquito likes to drink warm human blood. But, while they drink our blood, some species of Anopheles can also pass on deadly malaria. This disease has killed more people than any other on our planet.

FACT: Each female mosquito takes just a tiny drop of bright red blood.

DANGER

The Anopheles mosquito has a tiny microbe living in its body, this microbe is conveyed with anticoagulants in the saliva and injected into the host when the mosquito bites. In some cases, this microbe can cause the killer disease malaria.

LETHAL POWER

Taking a tiny amount of blood causes no problem at all. But malaria has killed hundreds of millions of people throughout human history.

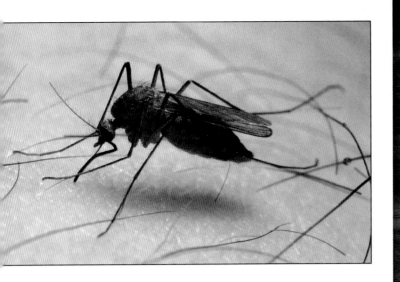

ATTACK

A female mosquito does not bite with teeth. It has a feeding tube like a hollow needle. It jabs this tube into human skin to suck up blood.

SHAPE

A fully grown mosquito has two scaled wings, a slender body and six long legs. They can vary in size but are rarely larger than 15 millimetres.

PREY

Female mosquitoes are only interested in drinking the blood of mammals – humans are easy targets. Mosquito adults also feed on flower nectar and juices of fruits for flight energy.

DEADLY SCORES

Hard to see, the Anopheles mosquito is not a likely killer, but it can carry deadly parasites responsible for millions of human deaths.

SHAPE
2/10

DANGER
9/10

ATTACK
6/10

LETHAL POWER
10/10

PREY
9/10

DEADLY TOTAL
36/50

Beaked Sea Snake

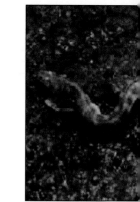

The beaked sea snake lives in the Persian Gulf and in the waters surrounding the Philippines and North Australia. This sea snake is a bad-tempered killer. This one species is responsible for about half of all sea snake attacks and for 90 per cent of deaths from sea snake bites. Its venom is deadlier than that of most of its land counterparts.

ATTACK

Sea snakes have much shorter fangs than land snakes – just 2-4 millimetres long – but they are just as sharp and deadly. The venom of the beaked sea snake acts very quickly.

LETHAL POWER

The venom is the sixth most deadly of any snake's in the world. It attacks the muscles and stops the victim from breathing, which quickly causes death. Just one drop of venom is enough to kill three men.

DANGER

The beaked sea snake is often caught in fishing nets. People trying to take the snakes out of the nets are the ones most likely to get bitten. The beaked sea snake is responsible for more than half of all cases of sea snake bites.

PREY

The beaked sea snake can swallow a prey twice the size of its neck.

FACT: Vivid black markings make this deadly sea snake easy to identify.

SHAPE

This snake can reach a length of up to 1.3 metres. They have specialised flattened tails for swimming and veils over their nostrils which are closed in water.

FACT: These snakes are able to dive up to 100m and stay underwater for up to 5 hours before re-emerging.

DEADLY SCORES

An aggressive and bad-tempered reptile with sharp fangs and deadly venom – the beaked sea snake would not make a good pet.

SHAPE
7/10

DANGER
8/10

ATTACK
8/10

LETHAL POWER
8/10

PREY
6/10

DEADLY TOTAL
37/50

Sea Wasp Jellyfish

The final verdict – no living creature is more deadly than the Indo-Pacific Sea Wasp Jellyfish. This small, boneless animal is found in the seas around Australia. It has dozens of stinging tentacles armed with a deadly venom that kills almost instantly. Worse still, this transparent and colourless jellyfish is almost impossible to spot under water.

ATTACK

Every tentacle has about 500,000 tiny, coiled stinging cells, each one with a sharp point. These cells are triggered by the slightest touch and inject deadly venom into the victim.

DANGER

Hundreds of people are stung every year, and many die. To protect people, many beaches in Australia are closed when there are sea wasps about.

SHAPE

It has a roughly four-sided shape (it is also known as the box jellyfish) and grows to about 30 centimetres in width, with tentacles that are up to 3 metres long.

FACT: *The white blobs on the tentacles are clusters of tiny, spring-loaded stinging cells.*

LETHAL POWER

Sea wasp victims feel a sudden burning pain and the venom may stop the heart from beating within a few minutes. A single Indo-Pacific sea wasp carries enough venom to kill about 50 human beings.

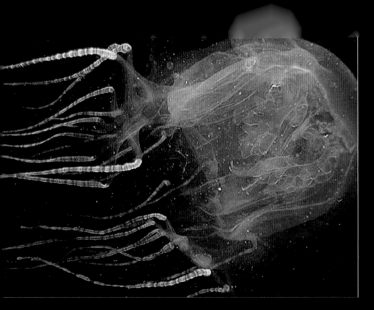

T: All jellyfish have a soft, hollow body.

PREY

The sea wasp feeds mainly on shrimp and small fish.

DEADLY SCORES

Not just deadly, this creature is almost impossible to see, which is another reason to avoid it at all costs!

SHAPE
10/10

DANGER
10/10

ATTACK
6/10

LETHAL POWER
8/10

PREY
7/10

DEADLY TOTAL
41/50

CLOSE, BUT NOT CLOSE ENOUGH

Before deciding our Top Ten Lethal Killers, we also considered these animals – all of them are deadly killers, but not quite deadly enough to make the Top Ten.

CONE SHELL

The cone shell is a kind of marine gastropod (sea snail). There are various species, with shells ranging in size between 3 and 11 centimetres, often brightly coloured. If you saw one on a beach, you might be tempted to pick it up – bad move! All cone shells can inflict a painful sting and some species also inject a deadly toxin.

GILA MONSTER

This strange-looking reptile is one of only two venomous lizards in the whole world – and they both live in the deserts of the south-western USA and northern Mexico. The Gila monster does not have two long fangs to injects its venom, like poisonous snakes. Instead, it has short teeth, but they are all venomous, and the venom is strong enough to kill an adult human.

STINGRAY

The stingray is closely related to sharks, but you do not have to worry about its bite — it's the sting in the tail that's the problem. This fish likes shallow water, and often hides in the sand on the seabed. Unwary swimmers and paddlers are liable to be speared by the long, venomous spine that is located near the base of the stingray's long tail.

HARVESTER ANT

Harvester ants are common in the United States of America. They like to collect plant seeds without any disturbance. If any human being gets in their way — maybe while having a picnic — then they ought to watch out! Harvester ants are equipped with a sharp sting that injects dangerous venom. Pain and itching are immediate, and death sometimes follows.

WESTERN DIAMONDBACK RATTLESNAKE

The Western Diamondback is the strongest and most aggressive of the North American rattlesnakes. This highly dangerous snake prefers to keep its venom for prey that is small enough for it to swallow. Large intruders are warned by the distinctive rattle, and they had better beware — this killer bites fast and bites deep.

Fierce Predators
INTRODUCTION

This section is a catalogue of the world's Top Ten predators. Predators are natural born killers, it is what they do – they must kill in order to eat. There are many different animals that are predators, including mammals, birds, reptiles and fish. But which is the best? Our Top Ten predators were rated according to:

SPEED

High speed gives a predator a tremendous advantage. The cheetah, which is the world's fastest animal, was clearly the winner in this category. With the others, we also looked at whether the animals could leap, and how far. We also gave extra points to crocodiles because they can move on land as well as in water.

BODY MASS

Size is obviously important for a predator. The bigger the predator, the bigger the prey it can attack. Weight is also a key factor as, a heavy predator will find it easier to drag down and overpower its prey. We gave our predators a combined score based on their size and weight, but we also took into consideration the average size of their prey.

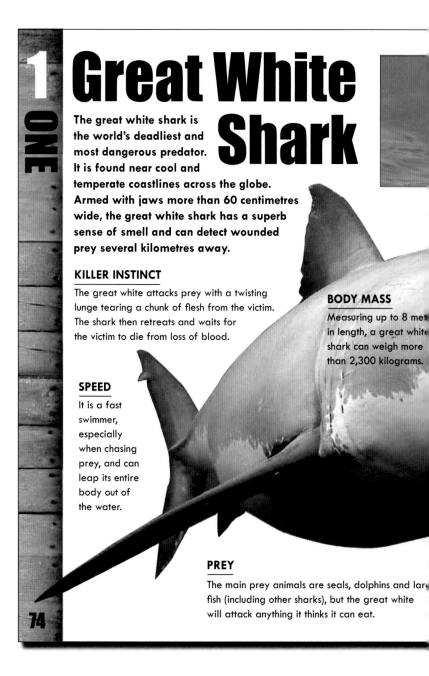

1 ONE
Great White Shark

The great white shark is the world's deadliest and most dangerous predator. It is found near cool and temperate coastlines across the globe. Armed with jaws more than 60 centimetres wide, the great white shark has a superb sense of smell and can detect wounded prey several kilometres away.

KILLER INSTINCT
The great white attacks prey with a twisting lunge tearing a chunk of flesh from the victim. The shark then retreats and waits for the victim to die from loss of blood.

BODY MASS
Measuring up to 8 met in length, a great white shark can weigh more than 2,300 kilograms.

SPEED
It is a fast swimmer, especially when chasing prey, and can leap its entire body out of the water.

PREY
The main prey animals are seals, dolphins and lar fish (including other sharks), but the great white will attack anything it thinks it can eat.

74

KILLER INSTINCT

Here we look at the overall style of each predator's attack. We gave points for hunting technique, stealth and camouflage. Additional points went to those predators that were able to achieve the all-important element of surprise, taking their prey unawares. Animals with highly developed senses for locating prey were awarded bonus points.

TEETH AND CLAWS

This category examines the tools of the predators' trade – the deadly weapons that are used to kill their prey. We based our score on the number, length and sharpness of the teeth and claws of each predator. These scores were adjusted according to whether it is the teeth or the claws that are the primary offensive weapons.

FACT: These teeth are designed to slice rather than grip. Each tooth lasts for less than a year before being replaced by a fresh one.

DEADLY SCORES

Among the largest underwater predators, thanks to his varied attack technique the white shark is also one of the most efficient hunters on Earth.

SPEED
4/10

BODY MASS
9/10

KILLER INSTINCT
10/10

TEETH AND CLAWS
10/10

PREY
10/10

DEADLY TOTAL
43/50

75

TEETH AND CLAWS

ws of triangular teeth line the great ite's massive jaws. Each tooth is serrated e a steak knife and is razor sharp.

PREY

Few predators specialise in just one kind of prey. Most are generalists that will attack anything that they can kill and eat – especially if they have not eaten for some time and are very hungry. Points were allocated according to the size and variety of prey that is normally taken. Extra points went to those predators that sometimes feast on human flesh.

Leopard

The leopard is a secretive and deadly predator that only comes out to hunt at night. Powerful limb and neck muscles make it the strongest climber of the big cats. The leopard lives in warm and cool climates throughout Asia and Africa, and is found in both open country and dense forest.

KILLER INSTINCT

This big cat may sneak up on its prey through tall grass. Or it may wait in ambush on a tree branch, before jumping down to sink its teeth into its victim's neck.

BODY MASS

The male specimen of this agile hunter weighs about 65 kilograms. Most leopards have pale fur with black spots, but some are entirely black. These black leopards are known as panthers.

FACT: Spotted fur provides excellent camouflage when stalking prey.

SPEED

Very few people have ever seen a leopard run at top speed, but it can reach about 60 km/h and can leap across a 6-metre-wide gap.

PREY

Although it can attack and kill larger prey, the leopard mainly hunts smaller mammals such as antelope, deer and wild pigs.

FACT: Eyes positioned at the front of the head indicate that this animal is a predator.

TEETH AND CLAWS

The leopard has broad paws with curved claws that end in very sharp points. Their massive skull presents powerful jaw muscles and long canines.

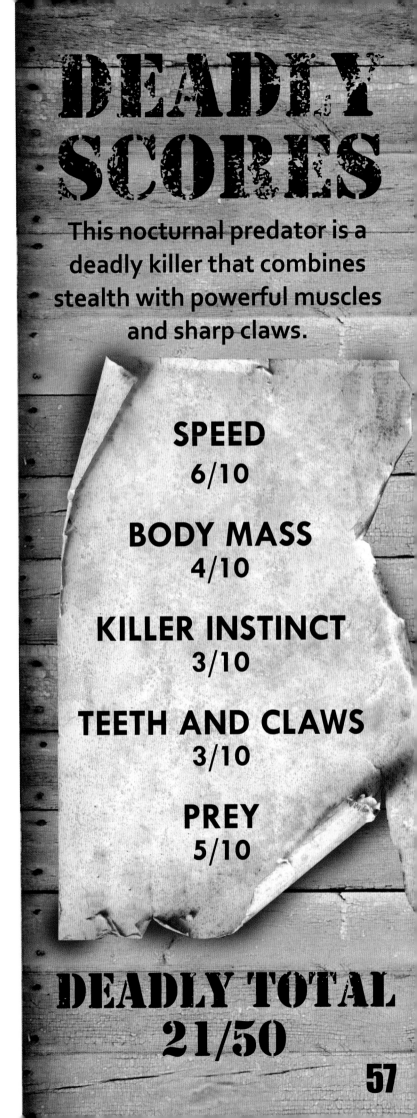

DEADLY SCORES

This nocturnal predator is a deadly killer that combines stealth with powerful muscles and sharp claws.

SPEED
6/10

BODY MASS
4/10

KILLER INSTINCT
3/10

TEETH AND CLAWS
3/10

PREY
5/10

DEADLY TOTAL 21/50

Coyote

The coyote is a North American wild dog that has adapted to a wide variety of environments. It is found from the hot deserts of Mexico to the frozen forests of Alaska and northern Canada. The coyote is a highly efficient predator that hunts by night and day.

KILLER INSTINCT

The coyote usually hunts alone, and can chase prey over long distances without getting tired. It has an excellent sense of smell for sniffing out prey hiding underground.

TEETH AND CLAWS

Its claws are sharp, but teeth are the coyote's main weapons. There are 42 in all, including four long, pointed canine teeth.

BODY MASS

The coyote is about the size of a German Shepherd dog, but much slimmer. The average coyote weighs about 14 kg and the male is slightly heavier than the female.

SPEED

Coyotes can run at speeds of up to 65 km/h for short bursts but can maintain a 32 km/h lope for long periods.

FACT: *Parents fetch food for young coyote pups.*

PREY

The coyote hunts a wide variety of prey; mainly small mammals, such as mice, rabbits and squirrels, but also birds, snakes and lizards. It will also kill cats and dogs in urban areas.

FACT: *A coyote uses its eyes, ears and nose to locate prey.*

DEADLY SCORES

Snow, rock, grassland or desert – it's all the same to this adaptable predator.

SPEED
9/10

BODY MASS
2/10

KILLER INSTINCT
4/10

TEETH AND CLAWS
6/10

PREY
2/10

DEADLY TOTAL 23/50

Polar Bear

The polar bear lives in the Arctic region surrounding the North Pole. It is the largest and most powerful predator that lives on land, and it has nothing to fear — except hunger. During the summer and early autumn, they often go hungry as they cannot hunt for seals when the sea is not frozen. Instead, they live off their fat reserves for months.

KILLER INSTINCT

The polar bear usually catches seals when they are out of the water or come to the surface to breathe. Sometimes a polar bear will break through ice to get at seal pups in their dens.

SPEED

A polar bear can run across snow and ice at speeds of up to 40 km/h. It is also an excellent swimmer.

PREY

While they mostly feed on seals, polar bears also prey on fish, seabirds, walruses and reindeer.

TEETH AND CLAWS

It has long, sharp claws that can easily rip through skin and muscle. Its powerful jaws can crunch through bones.

FACT: Powerful muscles are the key to the polar bear's deadly attack.

BODY MASS

A polar bear has a huge body covered in shaggy fur. It can weigh up to 800 kilograms and is more than 3 metres long.

FACT: Pale fur provides camouflage against the snow-covered landscape.

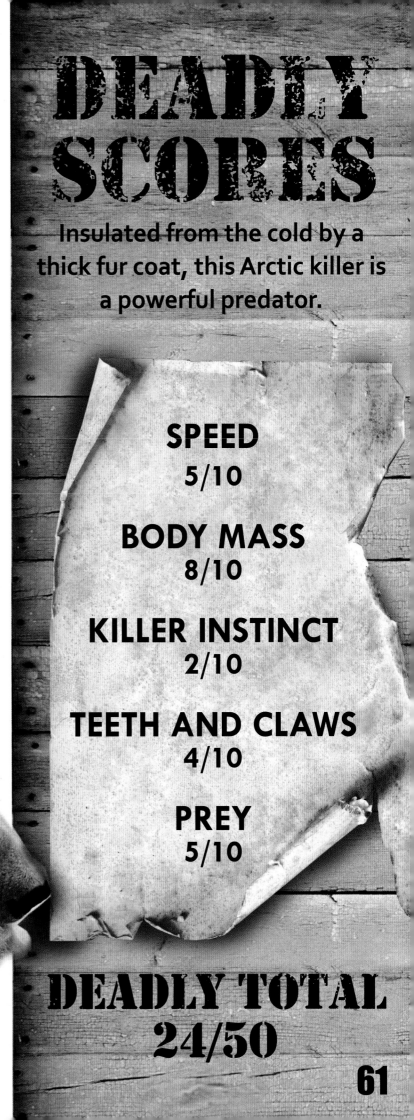

DEADLY SCORES

Insulated from the cold by a thick fur coat, this Arctic killer is a powerful predator.

SPEED
5/10

BODY MASS
8/10

KILLER INSTINCT
2/10

TEETH AND CLAWS
4/10

PREY
5/10

DEADLY TOTAL
24/50

Royal Bengal Tiger

The Royal Bengal tiger is one of the largest of the tiger sub-species and it rivals the Siberian tiger for the title "Biggest of the Big Cats". The Royal Bengal tiger is native to the Indian subcontinent but is now considered endangered. Like all tigers, it is a deadly predator and it can develop a taste for human flesh.

KILLER INSTINCT

Royal Bengal tigers leap onto their prey, digging in with their claws to drag their victim to the ground and biting their throats to kill them.

BODY MASS

The Royal Bengal tiger is the second largest tiger in the world. A male tiger weighs 200-250 kilograms and can measure up to 3 metres in length including the tail.

FACT: Tigers have spectacular vision: they can see six times better than humans.

SPEED

This tiger is one of the fastest animals in the world. They can only sprint for a short distance, but these tigers can reach speeds of nearly 60 km/h.

TEETH AND CLAWS

The Royal Bengal tiger has strong, sharp claws and powerful jaws equipped with 30 sharp teeth. It has the biggest canine teeth among the big cats.

FACT: *No two tigers have exactly the same pattern of stripes.*

PREY

This tiger will attack animals larger than itself and its main prey is deer. It can eat more than 25 kilograms of meat in one night.

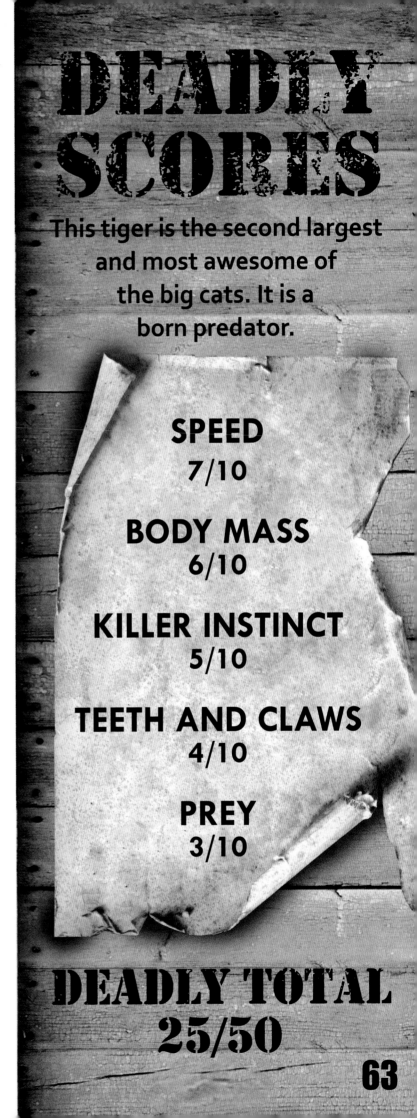

DEADLY SCORES

This tiger is the second largest and most awesome of the big cats. It is a born predator.

SPEED
7/10

BODY MASS
6/10

KILLER INSTINCT
5/10

TEETH AND CLAWS
4/10

PREY
3/10

DEADLY TOTAL
25/50

Cheetah

The cheetah is the fastest thing on four legs – it can run quicker than any other animal on Earth. The super-fast cheetah is one of the smallest of the big cats, but it is also one of the deadliest. The cheetah lives on the grasslands of Africa, where it uses its speed to catch fast-running prey.

FACT: *Sharp claws and teeth drag down a helpless victim.*

SPEED

Over short distances a cheetah can reach a speed of nearly 110 km/h.

FACT: *The cheetah has a very distinctive body shape, built for speed.*

BODY MASS

The cheetah has a slim, lightweight body and weighs between 35 and 70 kilograms.

KILLER INSTINCT

A cheetah usually hunts at sunrise and sunset. It will stealthily creep through the grass until it is close enough to its prey to launch a high-speed attack.

TEETH AND CLAWS

The cheetah attacks with both teeth and claws in a highly efficient "catch and cling" technique.

PREY

The cheetah hunts rabbits and small mammals, but can also attempt an attack on a zebra when hunting in pairs.

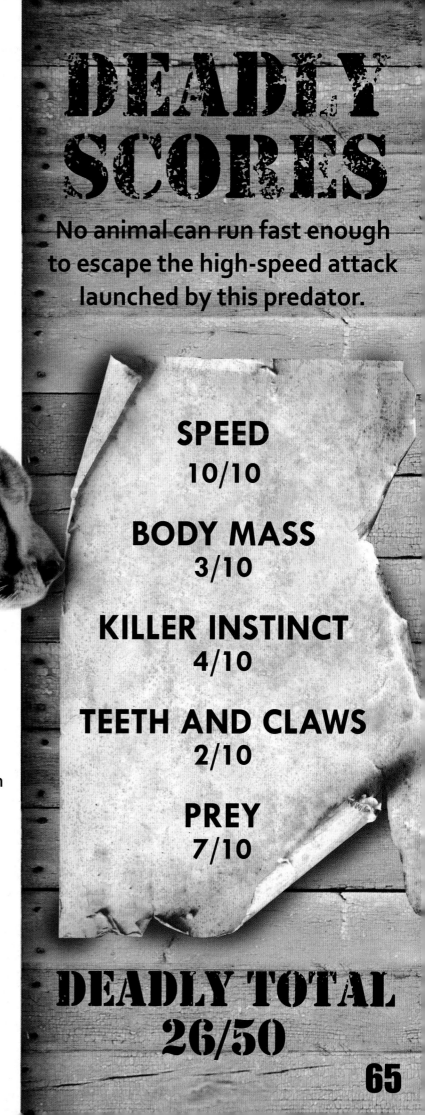

DEADLY SCORES

No animal can run fast enough to escape the high-speed attack launched by this predator.

SPEED
10/10

BODY MASS
3/10

KILLER INSTINCT
4/10

TEETH AND CLAWS
2/10

PREY
7/10

DEADLY TOTAL
26/50

Great Horned Owl

The great horned owl is a deadly predator that can kill prey up to three times its own size. It is so deadly that it has earned the nickname "the tiger of the woods". The great horned owl is found throughout North, Central and South America, and lives in abandoned nests, trees or even caves.

BODY MASS

The great horned owl weighs about 1-1.5 kilograms and stands over half a metre tall with a wingspan of up to a metre and a half. Females are larger than males.

FACT: As their large eyes are immobile, the owls can turn their neck a full 270 degrees to see in other directions.

KILLER INSTINCT

The great horned owl is most active at night. They use their excellent sight and hearing to find prey. They are stealth hunters and dive down from high perches to snatch their prey.

FACT: The coloration of the feathers provides excellent camouflage against tree trunks and branches.

TEETH AND CLAWS

The great horned owl has no teeth, but it does have a sharp beak for tearing flesh. Its main weapons are the sharp pointed talons on its feet.

SPEED

This majestic bird has a maximum flying speed of 60 km/h. It attacks silently and without warning, swooping down from its perch to seize its prey on the ground.

PREY

A great horned owl is capable of taking prey much bigger than itself. Its diet includes small mammals like mice, rabbits, squirrels and skunks. It also eats birds like ducks and quails.

DEADLY SCORES

This bird is a silent killer that swoops down out of the darkness without warning.

SPEED
9/10

BODY MASS
1/10

KILLER INSTINCT
7/10

TEETH AND CLAWS
4/10

PREY
6/10

DEADLY TOTAL
27/50

Nile Crocodile

The Nile crocodile is found in rivers, lakes and swamps throughout most of Africa. It is a cold-blooded killer, but rather a lazy hunter. This large reptile prefers to lie in ambush, with only its eyes and nostrils showing above the river surface, waiting for prey to come near enough for it to strike.

FACT: A crocodile swims by using its flattened tail as a paddle.

KILLER INSTINCT

Like other reptiles, the Nile crocodile can bite, but it cannot chew. Small prey are swallowed whole. Larger prey are grabbed and dragged underwater to drown.

BODY MASS

Nile crocodiles can grow up to 6.5 metres in length. They are covered in natural armour made of bony plates embedded in the skin.

FACT: *These long, sharp teeth can inflict terrible wounds.*

TEETH AND CLAWS

Its claws are fairly blunt and are mainly used for digging nests in the riverbank. Long jaws full of sharp teeth are the Nile crocodile's main weapons.

PREY

Small prey includes fish and water birds, but animals as big as buffalos and giraffes are attacked when they drink or wade across rivers.

SPEED

The Nile crocodile swims at up to 10 km/h. On land, it can run at almost twice that speed.

DEADLY SCORES

It might look like a log of wood floating in the water – but it is actually one of the most feared of all predators.

SPEED
3/10

BODY MASS
7/10

KILLER INSTINCT
8/10

TEETH AND CLAWS
8/10

PREY
6/10

DEADLY TOTAL
32/50

African Lion

FACT: The lion is Africa's top predator.

This powerful predator lives in the open grasslands of the savannah or veldt. Lions are the only cats that live in group, or pride: male lions defend the territory, leaving the hunting to their female counterparts. A few females often cooperate to attack large animals, while the males follow the hunt at a distance before taking over the prey and eat first.

TEETH AND CLAWS

These lions have five claws on each paw. Their powerful jaws are packed full with 30 sharp teeth that can lock together like a vice.

BODY MASS

African lions can reach lengths of over 3 metres, and can weigh up to 250 kilograms. The male is larger than the lioness.

SPEED

The African lion is not a good or fast runner, but it can reach about 55 km/h over very short distances.

FACT: Male lions are the only big cats with a mane of long fur.

KILLER INSTINCT

Female lions usually cooperate with each other when hunting. They often follow the prey on a broad front or they encircle it at the wings while the central animals lie low.

PREY

African lions hunt mainly large mammals. Their prey include zebra gnus, impala and wildebeest.

DEADLY SCORES

The technique of cooperative hunting gives this big cat a deadly advantage over all the others.

SPEED
8/10

BODY MASS
6/10

KILLER INSTINCT
7/10

TEETH AND CLAWS
5/10

PREY
8/10

DEADLY TOTAL
34/50

Orca (Killer Whale)

Despite its common name, the orca, or killer whale, is closely related to dolphins and porpoises. This marine mammal is found in seas and oceans around the world, although it prefers cooler waters and is rarely seen in the tropics. The orca deserves its popular name because it is a deadly, top predator with no natural enemies.

FACT: The orca has a distinctive black-and-white coloration.

SPEED

Orcas are fast swimmers. They can reach over 50 km/h in short bursts when chasing their prey.

KILLER INSTINCT

Orcas often live and hunt in small family groups that are known as pods, and the members of a pod often cooperate while hunting. Individual orcas will even seize sea lions that are resting on a beach.

PREY

Orcas feed mainly on fish (especially salmon), but they also hunt dolphins, whales, squid, seals, sea lions, penguins and marine turtles.

TEETH AND CLAWS

An orca has 40-46 large, pointed teeth, but it cannot chew and has to swallow its prey whole.

FACT: *The smiling face of a born killer.*

BODY MASS

A fully grown orca normally measures around 7 metres but lengths of nearly 10 metres have been recorded! These whales can weigh up to 9,000 kilograms. Males are bigger than the females.

DEADLY SCORES

This is one of the biggest predators on Earth – about 9 tonnes of killing power.

SPEED
5/10

BODY MASS
10/10

KILLER INSTINCT
9/10

TEETH AND CLAWS
9/10

PREY
9/10

DEADLY TOTAL
42/50

Great White Shark

The great white shark is the world's deadliest and most dangerous predator. It is found near cool and temperate coastlines across the globe. Armed with jaws more than 60 centimetres wide, the great white shark has a superb sense of smell and can detect wounded prey several kilometres away.

KILLER INSTINCT

The great white attacks prey with a twisting lunge tearing a chunk of flesh from the victim. The shark then retreats and waits for the victim to die from loss of blood.

BODY MASS

Measuring up to 8 metres in length, a great white shark can weigh more than 2,300 kilograms.

SPEED

It is a fast swimmer, especially when chasing prey, and can leap its entire body out of the water.

PREY

The main prey animals are seals, dolphins and large fish (including other sharks), but the great white will attack anything it thinks it can eat.

FACT: *These teeth are designed to slice rather than grip. Each tooth lasts for less than a year before being replaced by a fresh one.*

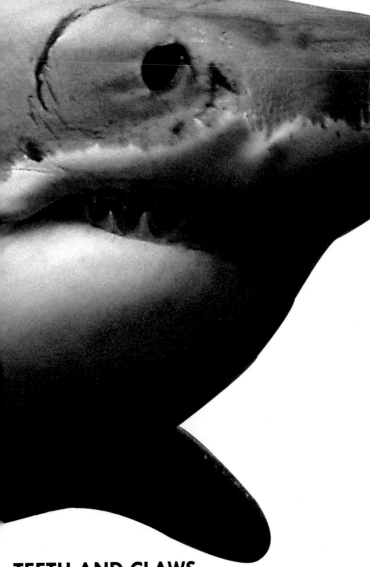

TEETH AND CLAWS

Rows of triangular teeth line the great white's massive jaws. Each tooth is serrated like a steak knife and is razor sharp.

DEADLY SCORES

Among the largest underwater predators, thanks to his varied attack technique the white shark is also one of the most efficient hunters on Earth.

SPEED
4/10

BODY MASS
9/10

KILLER INSTINCT
10/10

TEETH AND CLAWS
10/10

PREY
10/10

DEADLY TOTAL
43/50

CLOSE, BUT NOT CLOSE ENOUGH

Before deciding our Top Ten Predators, we also considered these animals – all of them are skilled and efficient hunters, but they are not quite good enough to make the Top Ten.

BALD EAGLE

The bald eagle is the national bird of the United States of America. It is not really bald, but the white feathers on its head and neck make it look bald from a distance. It is a large, powerful bird that weighs up to 6.5 kilograms and has a wingspan of up to 2.3 metres. The bald eagle is especially fond of fish, and swoops down to seize salmon in its sharp talons.

TARANTULA

Tarantulas are the largest of all spiders and they are widespread throughout tropical regions. The biggest tarantulas have a leg span of nearly 30 centimetres and can move very quickly. Tarantulas do not spin webs; instead, they are active hunters that prowl around at night looking for prey such as mice and small birds.

VAMPIRE BAT

This small South American mammal has a fearsome reputation because of its diet – it feeds on the blood of other mammals. The vampire bat does not actually suck blood; it bites its victim to make the blood flow, then laps it up with its tongue. Although it can fly, this bat likes to walk and it is more likely to attack its prey from the ground.

WOLVERINE

The wolverine is the largest and fiercest member of the weasel family. It lives in the coniferous forests of Europe, Asia and North America. The wolverine measures up to 1.3 metres from nose to tail, and weighs up to 30 kilograms. It chases after small prey such as hares and rabbits, and will climb trees to attack large prey such as deer with more ease.

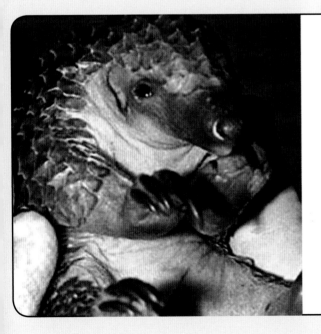

PANGOLIN

This strange scale-covered mammal is found in Africa and Asia. Although it is not at all fierce, the pangolin is in its own way a mighty hunter. It uses its powerful claws to burrow into termite mounds and ant nests, and then slurps up their tasty eggs with its long tongue. Its distinctive coat of hard scales protects the pangolin against ant bites and stings.

Glossary

Adaptable capable of adjusting to a particular situation or use

Agile able to move quickly and easily

Amphibian an animal capable of living both on land and in water

Antelope a fast-running, grass-eating mammal native to Africa and Asia, with long horns and a slender build

Anticoagulant a substance that prevents the clotting of blood

Antidote a remedy used to neutralise the effects of a poison or venom

Arctic regions around the North Pole

Bipedal animal that walks on two feet

Camouflage means of disguise by protective colouring or shape

Carcass the dead body of an animal

Carnivorous a meat-eating animal

Carrion the dead and rotting body of an animal

Cell the basic structure and functional unit of living organisms

Claw sharp, curved, horny structure at the end of a toe of a mammal, reptile or bird

Coral reef a reef consisting of coral – the external skeleton of a group of marine animals

Crest a tuft or ridge on the head of a bird or other animal

Cretaceous the last period before the extinction of the dinosaurs – 145.5 to 65.5 million years ago

Desert area of land that receives an annual rainfall of less than 25 centimetres

Dinosaurs reptiles that lived during the Triassic, Jurassic and Cretaceous periods

Fang a hollow tooth of a venomous snake with which it injects its poison, or a canine tooth of a carnivorous animal with which it seizes and tears its prey

Fossil evidence of past life – not only remains but tracks, burrows and faeces – that has turned to stone

Geologist scientist who studies the origin, history and structure of the Earth

Gland organ of the body which secretes chemical substances

Hadrosaur group of large bipedal dinosaurs with a horny bill and webbed feet

Heart organ that pumps blood through the circulatory system

Herbivorous a plant-eating animal

Jaws the structures that form the framework of the mouth and hold the teeth

Jurassic the middle period when dinosaurs were a dominant species on Earth – 199.5 to 145.5 million years ago

Malaria infectious disease characterised by cycles of chills, fever, and sweating transmitted to humans by the bite of an infected female Anopheles mosquito

Mammals warm-blooded animals with a covering of hair on the skin and, in the female, the ability to produce milk with which to feed the young

Microbe a minute life form; a micro-organism, especially a bacterium that causes disease

Nocturnal a creature active at night

Nostrils external openings of the nose

Omnivorous an animal that eats both meat and plants

Ostrich large, swift-running flightless bird of Africa. It has a long bare neck, a small head and two-toed feet

Palaeontologist scientist who studies fossils and related remains

Parasite an animal or plant that lives in or on another

Pincers front claw of a lobster, crab, scorpion or similar creature

Predator an animal that lives by attacking and killing other animals

Prey an animal hunted or caught for food

Protoceratops a four-footed plant-eating dinosaur with an enormous beaked skull that lived in North America and Mongolia in the late Cretaceous

Rainforest a dense evergreen forest occupying a tropical region with an annual rainfall of at least 2 metres

Reptile a cold-blooded animal that has scales and lays eggs on land

Saliva watery liquid secreted into the mouth by glands

Savannah flat grassland of tropical or subtropical regions

Scrubland an uncultivated area of land covered with sparse vegetation

Serrated notched like the edge of a saw

Shoal a large group of fish or other marine animals

Species a class of animals grouped by virtue of their common attributes and assigned a common name

Spine the series of vertebrae (bones) that form the axis of the skeleton and protect the spinal cord

Stamina lasting strength and energy

Sting a sharp, piercing organ or part, often ejecting a venomous secretion

Sub-species a subdivision (race or variety) of a species

Talon the claw of a bird of prey or predatory animal

Temperate describes a region free from extreme of temperatures

Tentacle a flexible organ near the head or mouth used for feeling or grasping

Theropod a carnivorous dinosaur with short forelimbs that walked or ran on strong hind legs

Toxin a poisonous substance that is produced by living cells or organisms

Tropical a hot and humid place relating to the tropics, a region on either side of the equator

Veldt open grazing areas of southern Africa

Venom a poisonous secretion of an animal, such as a snake, spider or scorpion, usually transmitted by a bite or sting

Venomous a creature that can produce venom

Index